Releasing Revelations

Adolph Moore

Releasing Revelations

Releasing Revelations
Copyright © 2018 by Adolph Moore. All rights reserved.
ISBN: 978-0-9907946-3-9

No part of this publication may be reproduced, stored in a retrieval system or transmitted in any way by any means, electronic, mechanical, photocopy, recording or otherwise without the prior permission of the author except as provided by USA copyright law.

This book is designed to provide accurate and authoritative information concerning the subject matter covered. This information is given with the understanding that neither the author nor MEP Publishing is engaged in rendering legal, professional advice. Since the details of your situation are fact-dependent, you should additionally seek the services of a competent professional.

The opinions expressed by the author are not necessarily those of MEP Publishing.

Published by MEP Publishing.
210 Riverview PL | Lillington, North Carolina USA
1.910.814.1554 | www.meppublishing.com

MEP Publishing is committed to excellence in the publishing industry. The company reflects the philosophy established by the founders, based on Habakkuk 2:2 *"And the LORD answered me, and said, Write the Vision, and make it plain upon tables, that he may run that readeth it..."*

Book design copyright © 2018 by MEP Publishing All rights reserved.

Published in the United States of America

TABLE OF CONTENTS

DEDICATION..4
INTRODUCTION....................................5
MARRIAGE 7
RELATIONSHIPS 19
LIFE..29
FINANCES...39
ENTREPRENEURSHIP........................47
FINANCIAL FREEDOM........................68
BUSINESS OPPORTUNITY..........68-75

DEDICATION

This book has been long overdue. Having said that I must dedicate my first book to GOD. God is the reason that I am here for such a time as this. I must thank God and dedicate this book to HIM. Secondly, my wife Erika T. Moore who has been by my side for the last 6 years and for that I am great full and thankful for her love and support. My daughter Charity Thomas for being there as well. There are so many to name, but without saying my father and mother Silas and Dorothy Moore, my brother Brad Corder for being my sounding board since 1996 at Ft. Shafter, Hawaii Brothers for LIFE. Lastly, everyone that came in and out of my life for a reason or a season I dedicate this book to you.

#CatchtheRevelation

INTRODUCTION

My name is Adolph Moore. I am a US Army Veteran, Husband, Father, Pastor, Mentor, Publisher, Entrepreneur and now Author of the first of many books to come. Some may say delayed, but I will say not denied. I started writing this book four years ago, but it is finally here. This book is going to bless you, encourage you, enlighten you, motivate you, and release in you a revelation that can and will change your life in every area of your life.

I believe I have been given a task from God to equip the people, not only the church folks, but the people 9as a whole.

Using the word of God, fasting, praying and mind provoking common sense are the tools that God has equipped me with to be a blessing to you today.

I am truly concerned with the total man (being). I believe that God wants us to be complete or whole in every area of our lives. I will focus on Relationships, Marriages, Success, Finances, and Entrepreneurship. We will deal with these topics in detail that it will help you and your family.

#CatchtheRevelation

Releasing Revelations

MARRIAGE

This is one of the best chapters in this book. I know right if you would have asked me twenty- five or thirty years ago you would have gotten a different response. In my early twenties, my mindset was being a player until the day that I died. I see that did not work out too well for me. I will be very transparent in this entire book. I believe everyone goes through a stage at every age in life. This doesn't matter if you are single or married. Most people do not know many scriptures, but the one that everyone knows is "Marriage *is* honorable in all, and the bed undefiled: but whoremongers and adulterers God will judge." Hebrews 13:4 (KJV) God honors marriage even when we don't God does. It is amazing how we lie on God regarding marriage. What do I mean? I'm glad that you asked. Many have, and many will continue to say that God said, or God told me to marry him or her. I always look for or at the fruit. When they break up, don't get married or get divorced, was that God's plan? We will revisit this later.

Earlier I mentioned that in my twenties my mindset was that I was going to be a player until I die. I thank God for the life that I lived. Not proud of all of it, but all of it made me who I am today. I will go in detail in another chapter. I will say this; you must get that out of your system before you consider marriage. All games must be played already. You must be ready to settle down and start, raise or become a family. Marriage is a serious vow made to God in front of your family and friends. I understand that all marriages do not work for whatever reason or whoever fault it is. This chapter is not to blame anyone or point fingers, but to learn how to be better and do better. One of my favorite quotes from me is **"Do not let Love, Lust or Loneliness be the reason that you sleep with, date or marry a person"**. Three top reasons people lie on God. Your emotions will keep you in trouble, keep you horny, and keep you in sin. Amen Somebody.

What needs to be the first rule or first nugget to have a successful or good marriage? **Put God first**. Invite God into the marriage. Another nugget is **praying together** as husband and wife. This will strengthen the marriage also. I have been asked this question a lot about dating. How long should you date before you get married? Before I answer this question, I will tell you what I have seen in the church first hand. Apostles, Bishops, Evangelist, Prophets, Pastors, and leaders have a date for up to five (5) years before getting married. Some of them lived together or what we call shacking. I will not call any names, but this is what the church is doing, so why would we expect something different from the world? Therefore, I stated you should get all the games, lust, dreams and fantasies out of your system. Get the threesomes and orgies out of your system. I know this is not popular and I expect people to say whatever they say.

Truth be told if they get it out before they get married, they have a better chance of staying married. I have always said, "The result of dating is marriage". If you are not ready for marriage, you should not be dating. Real Talk. Many church players male and female say that now they want to do a test drive before they get married. This is stated in the second or third week of dating. God help us all. Truly they do not want to get married. They just want sex. About to answer the question, how long should you date before you get married? When two grown people saved or not, church or not have themselves together mentally, physically, financially, and spiritually oh and sexually they are ready to date to Marriage.

The birthing process beginning to end is nine (9) months. I believe that two serious-minded grown people who are mentally, physically, financially, and spiritually, together can date to marriage in nine (9) months. My wife and I did it in seven (7) months and December 2019 was (6) years of marriage.

Marriage needs to be taught and branded as an awesome, noble and challenging adventure that it is. As a man, our manhood and happiness depend on our marriage. As men, we must understand that commitment is the key to success in marriage and life. Commitment will play a major part in your marriage. **One of my commitments to my marriage is that Divorce is not an option.** In marriage, it is the security of commitment that allows a woman to feel at peace in the relationship. The assurance of the commitment helps the wife entrust herself to him emotionally and sexually.

It's very important to make your commitment a priority. Not only does God honors marriage, but God honors commitment also. One of the number one problems in marriages is the fact that people do not commitment anymore. They will not wait or go through the testing process. Commitment means going through the highs together and going through the lows together. Commitment means through hell or high water I will be by your side. Commitment means through sickness and health I will be by your side. Commitment means richer or poorer, I will be by your side. Commitment and loyalty are rare components in marriages in 2020. If I do not know anything else in life, I know how to commit. If you commit to God and the things of God as husband and wife committing to God will be easy. Men we have committed to women who cheated, who lied and who stole. Women you committed to men who abused you, who played you and who brought nothing to the table. Why not commit to your spouse? Why not commit to your husband? Why not commit to your wife? I promise you, if the husband and wife, the man and the woman would commit today that divorce will never be an option and the devil will never have a place to stand in your marriage. Commit yourself to God and your spouse. #CatchtheRevelation

While commitment is very key to marriage also is communication. You will not have a successful marriage without communication. For a man, this may be a little challenging as far as the extent of communication. I have lived long enough to understand that men and women have different ways of communicating. Men are more visual, and women are more emotional communicators.

As men learn the language of how women communicate this will also break a barrier that has been plaguing marriages for centuries. I love my wife, but many times we cannot understand one another. Good communication requires trying to understand each other. The bible says in all thy getting, get understanding. What most couples will never admit is that they are married to someone that they are still trying to figure out and getting to know. No one gets married and knows everything about their spouse. **Good communication will unlock the mysteries of your spouse's love language. I know that sounds good, that got me excited.** Many times, we take our spouse for granted and will not tell them "good morning" or "good night" or "thank you". Good communication will keep the marriage happy. I strongly believe that happiness and marriage still go together. A strong indicator regarding communication is if your spouse did not talk in the dating stages why did you think they would talk after you got married. So many marriages end before they begin because love blinded them, and they could not see the signs. I will hit on the signs that we miss later. Good communication is also considered respect. When two people get married, it shows a sign of commitment, love, respect and a vow to communicate how they feel for one another. This is how you let your spouse know how to treat you, how to care for you and how to make you feel. I believe that 65% of couples fail to get a good understanding of what their likes and dislikes are and what their deal breakers may be. People are not candid or open for a real conversation about their expectations in a relation and marriage.

People are afraid to put it on the table. Can I say this for starters a relationship should never be 50/50? NEVER!!! ALL OR NOTHING!!!

Both people should come willingly bringing 100% of themselves, expecting the same in return. Society and Social Media have damaged the minds of people regarding expectations. When two people bring 100% to a relationship or marriage, they can be transparent, open and honest. Why would you date to marry someone, and you may only like sex once a month and your mate likes it three times a week. Can you see the confusion when they get married? When my wife and I dated we shared everything and I mean everything from sex, bills, money, sex, family, finances, likes, dos, don'ts, will and won't. Did I say Sex? Did I say Finances? These are the number one and two reasons couples fall out, argue and get a divorce. Talk about it before you say I DO.

The signs that good oral, good sex and good money cause you to miss. When they belittle, disrespect, verbally and physically abuse you, cheat, lie and steal from you and on you. When they do not bring anything to the table. I am very hard on men, so ladies if he does not have transportation, house or apartment, and employment or income, he is a NO GO. Run and do not look back. Seriously he should not be trying to date, he needs to be getting himself together is what I am saying. I never say this type of person is a bad man just not ready to date or marry. Women if you do not have your stuff together such as employment or income, transportation, or a place to stay, you are a NO GO also.

Men and Women, alike you must bring something to the table or relationship. Good looks and good sex alone will not and should not get it in 2020. Men if you are thirty (30) years of age and over you should not still be sleeping on your mama's couch and or dropping her off to work so you can keep her car to act like you are a "Mack." Listen marriage is designed by God himself, can we be honest about making it work. When people show you who they are and how they are it's up to you to accept the fact that they are not dating or marriage material. Many of you should be thanking God that you did not marry that Joker or that Jezebel that said, God, said you were their husband/wife. The devil is a liar and the truth is NOT in him or her. Shake the dust off your feet and move on.

Communication may be different at a certain age or stage in life. Men normally pattern after their fathers, not all just normal. As I look back to my childhood I cannot remember a lot of communication and affection from my parents out in the open. I know there was a lot behind closed doors because that where all old people conduct their business was in their bedrooms. From what I have noticed in life and my experiences is that men are not big talkers, but big thinkers. I believe if more men would have seen better or more communication between their parents especially their father, this would have been the behavior they pattern after. No excuse by any means. When you know better, you do better. As a man, I challenged myself to be a better husband and father than my father was. My father pushed me as a child to be the best at everything I set out to do.

I have been blessed with a father that has supported me in all my sports as a child. My father and I to this day have a three-dimensional relationship. He is my father, a brother and a friend. I owe it to Silas Adolph Moore that I am the father and husband that I am today, My Father and Mother Dorothy A. Moore has been married for forty-nine (49) years. I applaud them. Putting away all the childish things when you become a man, you learn how to be better and do better. We study for school, jobs, and sports, so why can't we study to be better communicators and listeners? I know brother Do little, this seems like work. Indeed, it is work. A marriage is a full-time job, it requires maintenance, tender, love, and care. Marriage requires monthly tune-ups, monthly oil changes, and monthly alignments. In other words, if you want your marriage to run smooth like a Mercedes Benz you must commit to ensuring that you both are on the same page. Sometimes it's the simple things like saying I love you every day, gentle touches and showing one another attention. Great commitment and great communication are two mandatory ingredients to a successful and happy marriage. There are no short cuts to the finish line. I told my wife "Divorce is NOT an Option". If God put us together like we said He did, that means it's going to require 100% from each of us to make the marriage work.

What if you have been married before? I am so glad that you ask. I have been married once before and I said I wasn't going to get married again because I was hurt. I felt like a failure. I did not get married to get a divorce.

I was saved when I got married the first time, but I cannot say that God put us together. I can be honest with you that you will reap what you sow in your lifetime. As I stated earlier in the chapter I got all the mess, fun and games out of me. I have done everything that a straight African American man dreamed of doing. I will go more in detail in the **SEX** chapter. My point is when I got married I was ready to settle down. I never cheated on my wife because I took my wedding vows seriously as I take marriage seriously. I am here to tell you that just because you have been divorced does not mean you are a failure. Divorce does not mean that you are a loser or cursed. If God does not put you together and if God is not in the center of your marriage do not expect it to last. Take the knowledge and wisdom that comes from the experience of going through a marriage that did not have a happy ending,

    I was saved and preaching and divorced and lonely. I was saved and preaching and hurt. I was saved and preaching and divorced and sleeping with women because I was lonely and hurting. I was bleeding and still leading. I was preaching in pain. I was to hurt to heal. I know firsthand how you can go from having breasts and thighs by your side to having an empty bed. It doesn't make it any better if you have a big appetite for sex. I ask God for many years why me? What did I do God to deserve this? I was mad at God and I was a mess. I was saved, sanctified, filled with the Holy Ghost and still fornicating, I stopped preaching because I could not continue to preach with that spirit in or on me. I know how single and saved people feel. After God revealed to me why I went through what I did.

God showed me why my marriage did not work. God healed my heart. God used my brother Brad Corder to get my attention. We had a conversation on the phone and I shared with him how many irons that I had in the fire. He repeated to me what I said, and it was like God telling me "Time to Stop NOW"!!!

That very day I repented again and got myself together and prepared myself for my wife. God restored my heart and soul. I never looked back. The power of prayer assured me to this day that God would never leave me or forsake me. As dirty as I was God took me back. His grace and mercy shall follow me all the days of my life. Why was I tripping? Let me tell you something the bible says "For a just *man* falleth seven times, and riseth up again: but the wicked shall fall into mischief. Proverbs 24:16 (KJV) We all will fall, have fallen in some area of our lives, just don't stay down. The devil thought he had me. But, God did not let me go. I am here to tell you that God is a way maker, a miracle worker, and a promise keeper. Despite a divorce, you are still chosen by God. Despite a divorce, you are still destined for greatness. Despite a divorce, you are still favored by God…

Marriage is about God, Commitment, Communication, Work, Honesty, Compromise, Loyalty, Trust, Order, Structure, and Love. Prayer is a weapon that will always work for you in every situation. There will always be disagreements and arguments but always practice forgiveness. Saying "I'm Sorry" will go a long way and mean it. If couples can pray for each other, then come together and pray together. This would strengthen the marriage where God is the head. The Bible says "Wives, submit yourselves unto your own husbands, as unto the Lord. For the husband is the head of the wife, even as Christ is the head of the church: and he is the savior of the body. Therefore, as the church is subject unto Christ, so *let* the wives *be* to their own husbands in everything. Husbands, love your wives, even as Christ also loved the church, and gave himself for it; that he might sanctify and cleanse it with the washing of water by the word." Ephesians 5: 22-26 Men the bible also says "Husbands, love your wives and do not be harsh with them." Colossians 3:19 (NIV).

People do not value marriage anymore. At one-time marriage was a well-respected institution between a man and a woman.

Marriage - "gameo" - "gem" – "TO FUSE TOGETHER."

GEM – diamonds, sapphires, emeralds, rubies are all products of heat, pressure, time and fusion. Marriage is the fusion of the distinct human elements into one. Believe it or not, a successful marriage has little to do with love. Love will not guarantee a successful marriage. Love can bring happiness, but it does not make a marriage work. Knowledge is the only thing that will make a marriage work.

This may be a hard pill to swallow but Love alone will not make a marriage work. Love should not be the only reason why you want to marry someone. If you cannot see yourself with a person every day for your entire life. Your destiny should betide or connected with the person you want to marry. This is the importance of being led by God or God connecting you with your spouse. Again I will say do not let Love, Lust or Loneliness be the reason why you want to get married.

I dedicated this chapter to my amazing, anointed, beautiful, sexy, stunning, gorgeous, captivating, sensational, radiant and ravishing wife.

RELATIONSHIPS

If we like it or not we are going to be involved in Relationships one way or another and it is nothing we can do about it. Let's look and see. Our first form of Relationships starts with family. I know what some of you may be saying. "I don't like my family" and that is okay. Relationships are good, bad and ugly. There are many labels as far as Relationships or different levels if you will. We had or have no choice who our family is? We all have family regardless of if we are in Relationship with them or not. I have found out through history and life experiences that you will have better or longer-lasting Relationships with those who are not your family and it is okay. We have been condition to have a closed, one-sided mind. Accept family as who they are, where they are and keep living. God's perfect plan has the right Relationship in place in your life. I believe our expectations of our families are much greater than our family members. Why do we even put this on them? Why, because they are family? Or because they are relatives? I found out that there is a difference between family and relatives. We even have families that are more like strangers because of a lack of Relationship. It appears that most families expect you to automatically have a friendship with no Relationship. I believe that this is most of the cultures, but not all. Most of you probably grew up hearing or even thinking that family is first. Right, that's another conversation. We could go on for days talking bad or even ugly about our families. That wouldn't solve any problems. So how can we solve Relational problems in our family? I am so glad that you asked. I am going to say communications is the first solution and this is not just for family but every Relationship that you have with anyone. I am still learning that in Relationships people do not want to hear or know the truth about them or anything. The human race thrives on saying let's keep it 100, but that is so far from the truth. When you hear about families the first thing comes to mind is "Secrets" or "Family Secrets" "Rumors" and so on. In a lot of families and cases, it's a **Mystery in History**. I know you can relate. In every family, there is an alcoholic, thief, liar and a molester. You cannot assume that it's always Uncle or Granddaddy because it has been proven that there are females equally with the same traits.

 What has held most families back is the fact that we do not talk or communicate about our issues or problems, but continue to allow the secrets and rumors to go on. I can see many families are still hurt behind the past generation's pain. That family generational curse will never be broken until the truth and or transparency comes from the family. We cannot continue to take these secrets to our graves. Healing is necessary for the Pain and for the family to gain Power to conquer those Demons. Many families are in pain, crushed, devastated by acts of other family members. No longer can we cover and protect this rude, cruel, inappropriate behavior. We must protect the innocent ones in our families.

Releasing Revelations

I have studied people my entire life. Being the only child gave me a challenging perception. The longer you live you understand that your family does not always be your relatives. In other words, your relatives can be like strangers, distant, and inactive in your lives. I have even got more love from the streets than family and church. We expect our family (relatives) to support us, like us and love us. Why? #Ponderthat for a minute. Relationship is the missing piece to the puzzle. If you do not stay in communication and relations with family they tend not to respond to you. If I do not know you, If I do not have a relationship with you, if we do not communicate? You see where I am going. There are many reasons why kids (people) do not know their cousins, aunts, uncles, grandparents. This may explain why you are connected more to your co-worker more than you are to your cousin. You spend more with our hairdresser than your aunt. You found loyalty at the barbershop and not at the family reunion. More respect at the Masonic Lodge than Uncle June Bug and Aunt Lying Lillie.

Trust, Honesty, Respect, Communication, Loyalty, Happiness, Compromise, and Safety are 8 things that we long for and need in Relationships. You would be blessed if you found all 8 in one person, especially in the family. If you find one of these characteristics in a family member or friend you should thank God. Remember this the same demand and expectation that you have on people they should hold you to it also. You cannot expect from people what you are not. #CATCHTHEREVELATION

I have had hundreds of co-workers in my life. You are probably saying that's a lot. I had my first job at the early age of sixteen years old. I worked at a fast-food place called Hardees's where I had developed a few Relationships at that time, but not in communications with any of them now. People come in and out of your life for a season, a reason and a lesson to learn.

Growing up as teenagers you develop many Relationships in High School and College. Some stay in contact and many do not. Out of the guys I grew up with, ran the streets with and chased girls with none of us are in communication or Relationship now. I am going somewhere just hang in there with me. All of us as teenagers were tight, close and best friends in High School.

In 1991 I joined the United States Army, so after all my training I was stationed at Ft.Lewis, Washington. Going through that training turns you into a different, a better, and sharper person with Character, Integrity, Respect, Trust, Zeal, and Structure. All characteristics you want in a Relationship, Friendship, Family, co-workers, and acquaintanceships. Ft. Lewis was a great assignment where I learn a lot about me, life, and what I wanted in life. I meet hundreds of people, great Relationships, Friendships, and co-workers. Out of all of those people at Ft. Lewis I can proudly say that I am in communications with a married couple that was my NCO's then and now they are Pastor's here in North Carolina. Pastors Jeff and Deanna McNair. I love you guys. You never know the plans of God for your life.

Throughout my life, I have had hundreds and hundreds of Relationships. I believe and it appears that at each stage of your life you have different or even new Relationships. This term can easily confuse people when I am merely only talking about Friendships. From the ages of 13 through 18 you have a set of friends, 19 through 25 another different set of friends. From ages and stages, your friends change.

My Army days were the best days of my life for many reasons. The military as a whole is a bond, family and brother and sisterhood. Most soldiers remain friends for life. You can lose contact or communication, but once you connect again you never miss a beat. The military puts people (strangers) together and turns them into lifelong friends and family because of the closeness, ages, stages, and environment.

Back when I was at Basic Training my bunkmate was Jose Sanchez from Puerto Rico. We were strangers then friends and battle buddies. We had to stay together everywhere we went at Ft. Leonard Wood, MO. Military life, like a lot of other groups, companies, corporations when the move you place to place you meet and develop new Relationships and friendships all the same.

My military career lasted over 8 years and I can honestly say that I meet some of the most amazing people from all over the world. I am blessed to have met three of the hundreds of people in my military career at Ft. Lewis, Washington, and Ft. Shafter, Hawaii that I am still in Relationship and communication with today. Shout out to Pastors Jeff and Deanne McNair here in Spring Lake, NC where they Pastor an amazing church and my brother from another mother Brad Corder currently in Daytona Beach, Fl.

Whodini made a song called "**FRIENDS**" in 1984. The chorus goes *"Friends, How many of us have them? Friends, Ones we can depend on. Friends, how many of us have them? Friends, before we go any further, let's be Friends"*. This song has so much value and meaning that most never really paid attention to because it was a great song. True friendship will last a lifetime. How many of us have that? How many of us have people or friends that we can depend on? You probably will use one hand and have many fingers left. The reality of it all the word friend and the meaning of friends are not the same. Remember the qualities or traits of a friend? They are Trust, Honesty, Respect, and Loyalty with Happiness, Safety, and Communication.

Do not be so in a rush to put a label on people calling them your friend. This one word that is used very loosely. **There is a process to be promoted to a friend.** Before you can become a friend you must be an Acquaintance. Acquaintanceship is the beginning stage where you get to know one another. There is no time limit on how long you stay there or move forward. The people at the grocery store, post office, gas station, dry cleaners and even most co-workers. These are people that you see daily or somewhat often.

These are people that you see in passing and most times you may know their faces well and never know their names or anything about them, but have great conversations. Acquaintanceship is something that is never labeled it is just implied a person that we know or that is "So and So." Acquaintance is people who will never come to your house and you will never go to their house or ever invite them to anything. It is what it is and to be honest, these are some of the Best Relationships. No pressure, no drama, no or little expectations. So who and where are these people that are acquaintances? I am glad you asked. As I mentioned before the cashiers at the grocery store, gas stations, post office and also co-workers, churchgoers, social club members, and social media. Yes, social media is the biggest platform for Relationships of Acquaintances.

One of the best things about this type of Relationship is that there are no expectations. When it is a pass and go, see you when I see type Relationship you can only expect what it is. **Most of our problems come when we start calling these people friends and they are only acquaintances.** This type of relationship is not designed to keep secrets or share private moments. Just remember that you are in control of who you bring in and out of your life. I suggest taking it one day at a time going one level to the next in the Relationship arena. Every Relationship has to start somewhere. Even if you have plans on marriage you have to seek, meet and greet. Another issue or problem is that how can you get married in 3 days or less. I understand that people do, however going from hey, how you are doing to acquaintance to spouse is Crazy. I will say it. Sad but true. This leads us to the level of Relationships called Romantic.

The Romantic Relationship should never start at that level, if it does the chances are very slim that it last. Just like building a house it must have a solid foundation. All Relationships that last have a solid foundation. The Romantic Relationship should be based on the qualities of the friendship foundation. The saying is that you should be friends before lovers or romance. I will go in more depth and detail in the chapter "**SEX**." I will share a few pointers dealing with Romance that I learned over the years.

The 3 C's in a Relationship are Commitment, Communication, and Courtship. I will not break these down but these 3 C's are necessary to have a great Romantic Relationship. I will go into communication a little because this is the single thing all Relationships must have to be successful. What kind of communication does a romantic Relationship have? I am so glad that you asked. When I was dating Pastor Erika she was in Long Island, New York and I was still here in Lillington, NC. That meant communication was very important. There is a difference between communication and **Intellectual Stimulating Conversation** (ISC). ISC will leave an impact and impression on the mind, soul, and body of the person you are in a Relationship with. Not just a regular talk. I often refer to it as Mental Gymnastics. Your foundation must be solid and the ISC is the concrete. We must keep it alive and real in all communications when you take your Relationship to the Romantic level. It must be Intellectual and have intimacy to have Romance. Many will miss the ISC and intimacy and confuse it with something physical (SEX). The two are not the same but common feelings.

Relationships are not always healthy some are very toxic and dangerous. I will say this and be clear if he or she is putting their hands on you and it is not in a Romantic way you need to leave. Physical and verbal abuse is unacceptable. Love is not abusive nor would God be in an Abusive Relationship. The will of God is not for you to endure abuse or for you to stay in an Abusive Relationship. The Devil is a Liar.

Traditionally there are things that we copy or pattern after our parents or what we thought was a good Relationship. All problems cannot be fixed. All conflicts cannot be resolved. It is a myth or an illusion if you think that you can fix all Relational ship problems and conflicts. I have learned sometimes trying to resolve a conflict can cause more issues and problems than it fixes. Some battles are not worth fighting. Every Relationship is different and from my experience, it also depends on the environment that you and your spouse were raised in or exposed to. Sometimes it is okay to let some conflicts go unresolved.

Another situation that could become an issue is being willing to hurt each other's feelings. In our Relationships we say we want the truth, but we do not. Should a person be penalized for telling the truth if it hurts the other one's feelings? For example, if I am about to leave the house with a shirt that is too little and I ask my wife, baby how does this shirt look? Her reply is "That shirt is too small, you have gained weight and your stomach is showing." I cannot get made it is the truth. It needs to go both ways in a relationship, Right? Right! Men and Women are so sensitive about a lot of issues especially weight or appearance.

Spending time apart is a good thing in a Relationship. Tell the truth. Everyone needs some "ME' time or time alone. You should never put any pressure on a person you are in a Relationship with that they have to spend every second up under you or together. That is the control for one, two it is an insecurity issue. To remain true to who you are as a person you need to continue to do the same things that interest you. It is okay to have things you are interested in that your spouse or partner is not. When you were single you enjoyed taking long drives by yourself, you should continue if you like and if you need to. I have always heard that absence makes the heart grow fonder. I believe it is healthy to occasionally spend time from your partner. Understand you continue to communicate you will let them know what you are doing. I love my wife to life, but I love my time to myself also and I am okay when she needs time to herself. It is a beautiful thing when two come together as one.

REMEMBER WHAT MADE YOU, YOU!

#CATCHTHEREVELATION

LIFE

Releasing Revelations about Life. The bible tells us that Death and Life are in the power of your tongue. You can truly have the Life that you desire if you want it. One of my favorite scriptures is John 10:10" The thief does not come except to steal, and to kill, and to destroy. I have come that they may have *LIFE*, and that they may have *it* more abundantly." So I want to talk to you about living a more abundant life, living your best life, a purposed driven life. Everyone is talking about the 2020 vision because it is the year 2020. Yes, it is the year 2020 so you should declare this is your year to live your best life. Facts are your vision has not changed, but your life can change. You may be asking yourself how? What do I have to do? I am glad that you asked. Follow along with me if you can. Ask yourself if you are ready 100% for a change? Ask yourself what are you willing to do to change? Ask yourself what are you willing to do for a change? What are you willing to sacrifice? What are you willing to give up completely? You need to answer all these questions. I will wait......

    Let us start this journey together. Today is a new day. Today and every day of my life will be different. I will start my day off with prayer. Okay, let me set some guidelines to help you.

Before you check your phone, before social media, before you do anything. Give God his time first. Your first ten to twenty minutes of the day and then read scriptures that line up with where you are going or what you need from God. A good example is healing, finances, wealth, faith, patience scriptures. The next thing you should do is speak over your Life with Confessions or Affirmations. I like to say "Speak Life, Walk Faith" is what I coined. Let me show you and feel free to use this:

I AM THE HEAD AN NOT THE TAIL.

I AM MORE THAN A CONQUEROR.

GREATER IS HE WHO IS IN ME THAN HE WHO IS IN THE WORLD.

MY GOD IS BIGGER THAN MY PROBLEMS

I SHALL BE SUCCESSFUL

MY LIFE HAS PURPOSE

I WILL BREAK THE GENERATIONAL CURSE

I WILL NOT FEAR, WORRY OR DOUBT

MY GOD WILL AND SHALL SUPPLY MY EVERY NEED ACCORDING TO HIS RICHES IN GLORY THROUGH CHRIST JESUS

THE LORD IS MY SHEPHERD I SHALL NOT WANT, LACK OR GO WITHOUT

I AM A LENDER AND NOT A BORROWER

After this, you should be hype, fired up as I am right now. Now you should do somewhat we call personal development and motivation. I will list several that we listen to and like. We start every day this way and I do mean every day. You have to make a decision that your LIFE is going to change. YouTube "Bishop TD Jakes, Les Brown, Eric Thomas, Tony Robbins, Jim Rohn, Grant Cardone" These are just to name a few. These are great Life Coaches, Mentors and Motivational speakers. No matter what age or stage you are at in Life you will be able to connect. I am no way endorsing any one of these people or brands just stating that these are a few that we listen to on regular bases in the morning. Now that the first hour of your day has started, what's next?

"Speak Life, Walk Faith" is a lifestyle, not just a phrase. In spite of how our life seems to be going, we must "Speak Life, Walk Faith." Our life will be tested and tried on a daily bases. We must decide that we will be positive, focus, driven and have faith and not fearful of the unknown. Life I believe is designed to shape you and mold you into what your God-given purpose is. The shaping process is grimy, dirty and nasty in which no one likes or wants to go through. Often you hear the story of the Diamond of what it goes through to get to that final product. Nothing in Life starts in its final state or completed process. Just wait until you get to the final chapters of your Life, it gets better. I like to say "It gets Greater, Later," The Bible says "The glory of this latter house shall be Greater than of the former, saith the LORD of host: and in this place will I give peace, saith the LORD of Host." Haggai 2:9.

As I meditate on my Life and the different elements that will shape our lives are complex. There are so many variables and components to shape our lives and Relationships. Our life is never just simple. I believe people fine or can be fine alone with no drama. Once you add another person comes to the complications of Life. Being a male or female, then you have to be white or black, then you have been short or tall, then you have been skinny or fat, then you have single or married, then you could be rich or poor, then you could have education or not and believe in God or Higher power or not. You can have kids or no kids by the same person or multiple people. This is why Life can be complicated. In Life you almost must or have to deal with other people's emotions, issues, and problems. Most times it's hard to deal with your own.

Single life is a great life until you get married and then that becomes the Best Life. Stay single long enough to get to know yourself. Knowing who you are sounds simple. Knowing your will's wants, needs, emotions, goals, dreams, vision, purpose are just a few to mention. Career, family, and location are also things when single you may not think about. My recommendation is to stay single as long as you need or feel the need to. Marriage is nothing to rush or be pressured into. If you cannot care for yourself marriage should be the last thing on your mind.

My wife wrote a great book called 'Blending Fragments" which you must get after you read this book. Oh, wait, before you get that you have to get

"Sex, Lies & Church" to understand "Blending Fragments". The next section of this book will be about something in life that is more common now than ever.

    "Blended Families" are being born at a rate of 1,300 a day. Over 6 years ago we birthed our very own Blended Family. I will not go too deep into it, but deep enough to help someone see a different perspective. I believe most single men have not given it much thought about going into a Relationship with a woman with kids. What I mean by much thought is combining you and your kids if you have some with someone else kids. Normally your thought is about you loving the man or woman and their kids and becoming a happy family. I will go over the statistics later. Going into a Blending Family you must have great communications and plan about everything. What men forget the most is that her time is always shared. In the beginning, is never the way it ends or becomes. Family dynamics can vary in many ways. The mature adults in Blended Families do not use the word (Step). The parents are the parents and the kids are the kids. Just for this illustration, I will use (Step) to identify stepparents, step-siblings and or half-siblings that may be in the dynamics of your Blended Family. Multiple children and or multiple children's parents better known as Baby Mama (BM) and Baby Daddy (BD). When you meet him or her and you see that is what you like and after you spend time with them and you say this is what I want. You love the person and make a decision that I want to marry the person and you agree to accept (the package) the family also. That is why it is important to know who you are and to know yourself before you even consider marriage. 26% of children live in Blended families. 60 -70% of marriages fail that have children. What am I trying to say, "You must be mature and ready to be a father or mother? Just because he or she is fine and the body is banging and you want to hit it all day every day and all that is fine. As long as you have to be mother and father your needs and wants have to wait…Yeap I have learned myself more than I expected or planned.

      Here are a few common challenges that all depends on the ages of the kids, sex of kids and if you are relocating? Different traditions, adjusting to change of location, bonding, communication and compromising with parenting discipline style or lack of. Other common challenges are families or grown children who may live with your soon to be spouse. You can talk about this, men and women before the new husband and wife come the house needs to be in order. I will say this and I understand that I am not like most men. Being that I am an Army veteran of 8 years, traveled the world and other countries, a born leader going up, excelled in every sport and grew up fast having a daughter at the age of 16 years old. I am a stern, firm and no-nonsense kind of guy and I love my wife dearly and I knew that her order of the house and my order of the house were nowhere close. Some things cannot be compromised when you are the head of the house responsible for everyone's safety. Women never let your children rule your house especially if you plan on getting married.

I will say this, men and women. Love is good and it is great, but love alone is not a good enough reason to get married. Dating a single mother or father is honorable because you could be the parent to fill in the gap in the absence of the biological mother or father. Understand that every Relationship with the parents is different and some may be good and healthy and some not at all. The role of the new parent in a Blended Family is truly important for that reason alone. In a perfect world, you would believe that the parents would never abandon the kids or at least stay in their lives until they turn 18 years old. Our daughter will be turning 18 in 3 months. I can honestly say and not bragging that she has learned a lot from me. I taught her how to drive and she got her driver's licenses at 17 years old which is earlier than any of her older sisters. Now she plans to go into the military and make a career. My point is you never know what kinds of seed you are going to plant as the new parent. Any time you come with rules, chores, discipline, structure and a game plan you will be hated and disliked. Do not bend because it is a test to see if they can change or control you. Once they see they cannot break you they will fall in place. In my experience and studies, I found out that children desire discipline from their parents. Children want structure and order. They want stability. They want something that they can count on no matter what. The children that are over 18 years old are grown. The keyword is grown. They have no say so in your house with the new parent. This should have been established from the very beginning. I am reminded in the bible where it says "Can two walk together unless

they agree?" Amos 3:3. I will be very transparent. I have seen many marriages break up because of grown adult children and I always wonder how does this happen. Well again if I did not know who I was my wife grown adult children could have run me off. Being totally honest I started to leave several times in the beginning. I didn't sign up for the 4 grown adult children. My responsibilities were for my wife and the young teenage child when we got married.
Understand that being the voice of authority is never welcome in a toxic chaotic environment. Also, I clearly remember hearing one of the grown adult children cussing at my wife and I told them you will not talk to my wife like that in my house and they said they can talk to their mother anyway they want to. Do you see the problem or at least one of the problems? Men and Women, these are things you need to think about before you consider getting married. If your grown adult children do not respect you, they should **NOT** be living with you. That means physical and verbal abuse, disrespect and a lack of respect. Ladies, a Real Man is never going to tolerate that foolishness and not trying to be funny some men do not care. If your grown adult children want to be the boss put them out if you plan on getting married to a Man of Honor, Valor and Integrity. He will never want his Queen to be DISRESPECTED. I do understand all situations are different and LIFE happens and we let one of her grown adult daughters stay with us. She contributed and she followed the rules of the house. No problem after they saw that I wasn't going anywhere. I have no problems with any of my wife's grown adult children. I love them ALL…

I just wanted to share what people are afraid to talk about. I believe your transparency will lead to people's healing. People for some strange reason think what they don't know won't hurt them and that is the biggest lie on the planet. The bible says "My people Parrish or are destroyed because of lack of knowledge" Hosea 4:6. This tells us that because we don't know and do not try to know we are killing ourselves. Many of us have heard the saying "if you want to keep something from us, put it in a book." I am guilty myself I do not read like suppose or should. That is changing now as I finally complete this book. I have been writing this book for 4 years. I started, I stopped, I started and I stopped, but I never gave up. Winners never quit and quitters never win. You do not have to be great to start; you just got to start to be great. No matter how much you prepare yourself and practice you will never be perfect, but you will be ready. Stay ready so you don't have to get ready. As a boy scout, our motto was "Be Prepared." When you are prepared and ready nothing can surprise you or catch you off guard. *Guard your ears and eyes against everything negative so you will not lose focus.* Focusing on your goals and dreams will lead you in a forward and upward position. *Keep rising to the top and give it all you got.* True dedication requires discipline and sacrifice. Watching reality television and playing games will not lead you to any kind of success or will it help you attain any. The fear of the unknown has crippled thousands of people. Not so much the unknown just fear itself.

False Evidence Appearing Real. Now that I got your attention follow me.... #CatchtheRevelation

The thing about fear is that most of us do not know that we are living in fear. If you studied or pay close attention to what we say and what we do and how we act. I often hear Christians say "If the Lord willing about this or that." I always say if it is in the word of God, then it is in the Will of God. I have come to believe that most Christians are full of fear and negativity. Complaining and wining all the time is not the Will of God. I lot of what I see is passed down from generation to generation. Death and Life are in the power of your tongue and so is Fear and Faith. My saying again is "Speak Life, Walk Faith."

Just because it ran in your family doesn't mean that it has to keep running in your family. I do not want to call it a curse. I would rather say that it is time to serve notice to the devil. Fear doesn't live in you or your house anymore. The bible says "God did not give us the Spirit of Fear." We must believe and trust God. Side Note: **Don't say "fake it to I make it."** Think about it. This is one of the worst lies that you can ever say. God is not in it. Confess and Speak truth and life, not lies, fear, and deceit.

Your Life is not your own Life. Your life is to glorify God and show the goodness of Jesus Christ. We often ask ourselves WWJD. What would Jesus Do? You cannot expect God to bless you if your Life does not line up with the word of God. **Let your conversation be pleasing to heaven and God Almighty**

FINANCES

If you are like me, you have heard one of the misquoted scriptures in the world. Yea I know you only hear this scripture from broke Christians anyway. Money is the root of all evil. That's what we have heard our entire life. My point to bringing this out is if we will go our entire life based upon untruths or lies what else will we fall for? We will fall for anything or we will always be lazy and not do our research for ourselves. 1 Timothy chapter 6 verse 10 says "For the love of money is the root of all evil: which while some coveted after, they have erred from the faith, and pierced themselves through with many sorrows." I can honestly say that money is not the root of all evil. There are millions of things that are the root of all evil. Going further dealing with money or finances we should understand that we need it to live or survive. Most of us have had bad teachings our whole life and most of us are still struggling today. I just want to shine some light on a few things that could help you in life.

The principles never change, if saved or unsaved meaning if you are a Christian or not. My bible tells me He rains on the just and unjust. Why would the bible say, "Money answers all things"? Indeed. Just keep your priorities in the right place. God should always be number one.

I always wondered why a lot of non-Christians were millionaires or billionaires. That's when God showed me that the principles never change. You just got to use them. One of the best principles that will change your life is 2 Corinthians chapter 9 verse 7 which reads "Every man according as he purposed in his heart, so let him give: not grudgingly, or of necessity: for God loves a cheerful giver." This truly has changed my life. Eyes wide open to the fact that the more you give happily the more God gives to you. I have heard and believe this to be true that Bill Gates has given and donated so much money away that God has blessed him abundantly that he can't give all his billions away in his lifetime. WOW…. He has had to hire more people to his staff to delegate to give his money away. A great problem to have. There are hundreds of millionaires and billionaires who have this same problem. I pray to God that you too will have this same problem. Finances and money will not be your problem.

Start looking at your life as being a blessing to other people. Look at your life how you can serve other people. Look at your life how you can help other people. Look at your life as a problem solver. God loves a cheerful giver. I want your finances to become blessed. Give your money, tithe, talents and time. **ALERT!!!** You do not have to be a Christian to give your tithes, talents or time to God or the church. The tithe is 10% of your weekly, bi-weekly or monthly income before taxes.

10% is the minimum and you can always give 20% or 30% as you are led to do so.

Your talents are valuable also which you may call gifts. Your time has more value than you think.

Many communities and churches need volunteers, mentors, and helpers to assist the needs of the people. What does this have to do with my finances? **EVERYTHING**

Here are a few sayings that I live by:

"Refuse to go broke; trying to prove you're not broke to people who are broke"

" If you have never been at the bottom: broke, homeless, carless, jobless, hopeless, starving betrayed or counted out." You won't understand me.

"When GOD wants you to grow, He makes you uncomfortable"

"Eliminate everything that doesn't help you evolve"

"You can't have a million-dollar dream with a minimum wage work ethic"

"The average millionaire has seven streams of income…if your job is the only income you're hustling backward."

"If you don't learn how to get paid while you sleep, you'll work until you die"

"Either I will find a way, or I will make one"

"If you are persistent you will get it. If you are consistent, you will keep it."

"If you don't build your dreams, someone will hire you to help build theirs."

"But thou shall remember the LORD thy GOD: For it is He that giveth thee power to get wealth, that He may establish his covenant which he sware unto thy fathers, as it is this day." Deuteronomy chapter 8 verse 18 (KJV) Always remember it is God that gives us the power to get wealth. God gives us the power the ability and the ideas and concepts to get wealth or make money. I believe many church folks think that God is going to drop bags of money from the sky. NOT. Here are a few things that will cultivate and condition your mind to get in position.

- Disconnect from people and spend some alone time
- Learn new things to stimulate your thoughts
- Sleep well to rest mind and body
- Pursue your interests and exercise to ensure a healthy life
- Reading for leisure and spending quality time with family
- Stop complaining
- Stop blaming others
- Stop negative self-talk
- Stop dwelling in the past
- The need to impress others
- The need to always be right
- The need for other's approval
- Speak things into existence

I also like to say, "If you can't handle being talked about then you not ready for success." They will talk about you until the day you die.

A very key element is that you must be delivered from people and people's opinions of you. If you live long enough you will understand people will always have something to say about you good or bad. Truth be told more negative things will be said about you, your entire life. I suggest that you give them something to talk about. Some people say the best revenge is massive success. Not that it is revenge but doing well in life and knowing who you are and what the word of God says about you. Finances will not be your story or your problem in life.

I have Released several keys and nuggets to unlock new Revelations in your life dealing with your finances. At the end of this chapter, I will recap most of the keys and nuggets. One thing that I must highlight is that dealing with finances is how we were raised up or taught as kids. Most of us were told to go to school to get good grades and go to college and you would be successful or well off. Those four to six years of college turned into 30 years of debt. On the other hand, you never had anyone to tell you that you can start your own business or that you can be your own boss and be successful. This has a lot to do with where you are currently at now in your finances. Nevertheless, it's not too late in either direction that you decided to go. Entrepreneurs are those who may work 70 to 80 hours a week for themselves versus work 70 to 80 hours a week working for someone else. The rewards are greater being your own boss. I am experiencing this now as an Entrepreneur. I am making a living, Living. The average millionaire has at least seven streams of income. How many do you have? It's not too late to start. Just Do It!!!

Now that we know that having lots of money is okay. We have learned that money is not the root of all evil. We read that money answers all things. We read that God loves a cheerful giver. We even read that God gives us the power to get wealth. What am I saying? Finances should never be our problem. Keeping God first is our major problem. Understanding that God created us to be the head and not the tail. He created us to be successful and to have success in life and business. Jesus had twelve that followed him close that He taught and trained. Those twelve were Entrepreneurs. They had their own business that everywhere they went they could make money. That just made me happy right there. Male or female, married or single you should desire to be financially successful and wealthy. I believe that we can be healthy, wealthy and wise. If the bible says we can have it we should get it. Let's get all the knowledge and wisdom to attain it. My job is to Release all the Revelations. I must help you get to that place called there. I am truly excited about your future.

   I must share this story with you when I was in the Army stationed at Ft. Lewis, Washington. I was 19 years old living in the barracks with three roommates. On my wall locker, I had a picture of a 3 series BMW which was my dream car at that time. I look at this picture every day for at least three years. I had dreams and goals to one day have my dream car a BMW. At the time I was driving a brand new 1991 Ford Mustang 5.0 LX very fast car but wasn't my dream car. A few years went by and I did a Permanent Change of Station (PCS) to beautiful sunny Ft. Shafter, Hawaii a dream assignment.

It would be in the most beautiful exotic sunny Hawaii my dream assignment when I got my dream car. The funny thing about it was, the picture that I had on my wall locker was of a 3 series BMW. How about my BMW was a 525i black on black with chrome rims? Yes, God has been good to me way before I got saved. This was before I got saved. He rains of the just and the unjust. The principles work, you got to work the principles. Whatever it is that you desire at that time in my life it was a BMW since then Lexus, Mercedes, Cadillac, Mustang, and many more. Set your goals and your dreams. A person with no vision will die. Write your vision down and keep it in front of you every day as I did. It will surely come to past. Have a vision and have corresponding faith to go with the vision. The principle works, you got to work the principles. Start giving God 10% or start giving God 20% of your tithes and giving your time and talents (gifts) to God and your community and people in need. Watch things change in your life. Watch the hand of God move on your life. Watch your debts demolish, watch your bills get paid off, watch the mortgage get burned for your house, watch your marriage get stronger, watch your relationship get tighter, watch your finances increase to overflow. Watch God do it. I am speaking life over your life. Just walk it in faith. Speak life and walk faith. No weapon formed against you shall prosper, but you shall prosper in every area of your life. You shall reap the harvest that you planted seeds 5 years ago, 10 years ago, 15 years ago, 20 years ago. Your season is now. You shall reap what you have sown. You are in your due "Season". #CatchtheRevelation

FOR SPEAKING ENGAGEMENTS CONTACT ME @ 910-514-3448 OR 631-902-6606

EMAIL: adolphmoore71@gmail.com

Website: www.meppublishing.com

Website: www.adolphmoore.com

Website: www.6figureswithadolph.com

Releasing Revelations

ENTREPRENEURSHIP

I had caught the Revelation that I was supposed to an Entrepreneur at an early age as I look back over my life. As a young boy, I would cut people's grass in their yards for $10 dollars. I also remember making mixtapes in junior high school with admirations of becoming a DJ. I sold the cassette tapes, yes cassette tapes for $5 dollars a tape. At the age of 16 years old I started working a job at a fast-food place in Lillington, North Carolina. I had always had a hustling, making money spirit. I looked through my military records at the paperwork that I filled out entering the United States Army. I realized that my dream at the age of 19 years old was to become an Entrepreneur.

I tried many businesses while in the Military and after the Military, but nothing had seemed to work. Fast forward to October 16, 2018, I found an opportunity that changed my life. I partnered with a company that allowed me to be my own Boss and shortly after I could fire my Boss at the company that I was working for. I believe when you work for a company or any job and you hate going to work, it's time to start your own business.

Why is it that Monday morning's heart attacks increase by 35%? People hate their jobs but have no choice. 70% of workers want to be their own bosses, but they do not know how to get there. I was one of those people trying many different opportunities, but I never gave up. Never give up on your dreams, hopes, goals or vision. God has given you the power to create Wealth. We all have an Entrepreneurial spirit. Just learning how to activate it is our problem. We know we want more out of life, we know we need more money to survive and we have been trained that going to get a job was the only solution. Most or even all of you were told to "Go to school, go to college make good grades and get a good job." Now you have $40K - $80K in student loans. Student loan debt is worst than bad credit. When you look at it, it doesn't make sense. You will never become wealthy working a job; however, you will make the company, president and CEO very wealthy. They understand the game of leverage. Your time and efforts are making them money.

Everyone has an economy. The United States, Your state government, your town, and local city all have an economy. Well, guess what? Your household has an economy also. You and your household need a budget, finances, bills, debt and so on. It takes money to properly run your household. Here are more facts and stats. I found out in life men will lie and women will lie, but numbers do not lie.

78% of Americans live paycheck to paycheck. 50% of Americans have no savings account. 60% of Americans do not have $500 at any given time. 40% of Americans do not have $400 at any given time. Did you know that the average income in America is $50,000 a year which is considered middle class? The top 25% makes $90,000 a year, top 10% makes $140,000 a year, top 5% makes $190,000 a year and the top 1% combined income is $380,000 a year. America is the wealthiest country in the world.

The best way to get to our desired destination called Wealth or Financial Freedom is called Entrepreneurship. I like to say the Spirit of the Entrepreneur. Once you commit to being your own boss as you commit to going to work for someone else. You will soon see that there is **NO LIMIT.** You can build your own business as big as you want. There is no cap on income. We found the solution to everyone's problem. We started a home-based business.

      To build **Generational Wealth** and **Residual Income** and **Passive Income** you need a **Home Based Business** better known as **Direct Sales, MLM or Network Marketing.** It's safer to become an Entrepreneur than an Employee. We are wealth builders as God created us to be.

      You should look for a **Turn-Key** opportunity that has lots of **Training** and great **Leadership.** They must have a proven **System**, **Software** and **Strategies** that work. **More Millionaires** come from **Network Marketing**. The company that we partnered with has great **Products** and **Services** which we love, need and priced perfect so we can make profits. The company has great **Leadership** and **Management**. The company has a great **Compensation Plan** with multiple ways to make income and full-time income. Lastly, we have great Support, Training, Technical and Customer Service. We have a company within a Company. We have a business in Business. Our leaders are reachable, touchable and loveable.

Mr. Ivey Stokes, Mr. Alvin Curry, and Mr. Larry Gates are the founders of the company that allowed us to make Residual Income and taught us the Income Shifting Strategies.

Network Marketing makes $178 Billion a year. $71 Billion a year in paying commissions. That is $200 Million a day that is paid in commissions. WOW!

16 Million Americans are Network Marketers and 96 Million Worldwide. 82% of Network Marketers do very well. The most common issue or problem is that people think that it is a get rich quick program or scheme. Some even call it "one of those pyramid schemes." Honestly speaking if you look at it the pyramid is your job or company that you work at, The CEO or president is at the top and all the employees and at the bottom and the managers and supervisors are in the middle.

Now you see the truth. The bible says our people Parrish because of lack of knowledge. Some say when you know better you do better. Now I say this like my brother **Eric Mckinley "Properly Applied Knowledge is Power."**

Here are more statistics and numbers about Entrepreneurship. Please do not be scared. Life is too short to have regrets. Let's Do It!

According to the Score Santa Barbara January 28, 2019, 51 percent of owners of small businesses are 50-88 years old, 33 percent are 35-49 and only 16 percent are 35 years old and under.

· 69 percent of U.S. entrepreneurs start their businesses at home. According to the National Association of Small Business's 2015 Economic Report, the majority of small businesses surveyed are S-corporations (42 percent), followed by LLCs (23 percent).

While around 9 percent of all American businesses close each year, only 8 percent are opened.

· 51 percent of people asked, "What's the best way to learn more about entrepreneurship?" responded with "Start a company".

- 62% of US billionaires are self-made.
- In 2016, there were 25 million Americans who were starting or already running their own business.
- #1 reason why businesses fail is there's no market need.
- 60% of people who start small businesses are between the ages of 40 and 60.
- There are 582 million entrepreneurs in the world.
- 22.5% of small businesses fail within the first year.

- Studies show middle-aged men start the most successful businesses.

39 Entrepreneur Statistics You Need to Know in 2020 according to smallbizgenius
By [Dragomir Simovic](#) · August 5, 2019

1. 62% of US billionaires are self-made. (Wealth-X)

According to data from a 2016 research done by Wealth-X, there are 585 billionaires in the US. Only 20% achieved this status through inheritance, while the huge majority are self-made. This is probably one of the biggest incentives for young entrepreneurs who are just starting up. The remaining 18% became billionaires through a combination of inheritance and hard work.

2. 15 million Americans are full-time self-employed. (FreshBooks)

This number is according to the Fresh Books entrepreneurial statistics, which estimates that by 2020, America will have 27 million self-employed professionals. One in five workers plans to completely change her career once she gets into entrepreneurship.

3. 62% of adults believe entrepreneurship is a good career. (Babson)

There seems to be a growing understanding of the benefits of entrepreneurship among people across the world. According to Global Entrepreneurship Model entrepreneur's statistics from 2018/2019, more than half of people feel starting one's own business is a good career move. There may also be some misconceptions because an astonishing 40% of respondents think it's easy to start a business, and 49% believe they have what it takes to do it.

4. There are 582 million entrepreneurs in the world. (The Hill)

Although this is a significant rise compared to previous years, there is still quite a lot of room for improvement. Namely, entrepreneurship stats can help countries gain a better understanding of the market needs in certain areas and create a more fertile ground for this development. It is a great way to spot both the flaws and benefits of certain industries and act accordingly.

5. 26% of entrepreneurs say their biggest motivation for starting their own business was the idea of being their own boss.
(Guidant Financial)

What's more, 23% wanted to pursue their passion and 19% just did it because the opportunity presented itself. For 12% of entrepreneurs, corporate America was the biggest problem, while 6% decided to start their own business after being laid off. According to entrepreneur data, another 6% did it because they weren't ready to retire, and 3% were inspired by various life events.

6. 33% of entrepreneurs have only a high-school diploma. (Guidant Financial)

It may seem surprising, but a third of all small business owners never got any further than high-school. This is an inspirational piece of information for the majority of young people who are worried they won't accomplish anything without going to college. Altogether, 67% went to college, and 4% even managed to get a doctorate.

7. In Brazil, 53% of the entrepreneurs operate on their own.
(Babson)

Entrepreneur statistics from 2018 tell us more than half of business owners in the biggest country in South America don't have any employees or intend to hire any. With this number, Brazil is the world leader, leaving Madagascar a distant second with just 30% of solo operators.

8. The highest number of self-employed professionals (19.6%) work in the construction/trades field.
(FreshBooks)

It appears that construction is the most popular profession for entrepreneurs, followed by retail with 10.9%, real estate with 10.7%, and consulting with 10.3%. The creative professions are in 7th place according to entrepreneurship growth statistics, while marketing is at the very bottom with 1.7%.

9. With a Global Entrepreneurship Index of 83.6, the US is the best country for entrepreneurs.
(GEDI)

The Global Entrepreneurship Index (GEI) is a numerical presentation of the climate a country creates for the development of small businesses. This index takes into account numerous factors to create one comprehensive overview of the situation. Switzerland takes an unexpected second place with 80.4, followed by three English-speaking countries – Canada, the UK, and Australia. Chad is bottom of the list with an index of just 9.

10. 59% of entrepreneurs who apply for a loan use it to expand their business.
(Federal Reserve Banks)

Entrepreneur demographics for 2018 show us 43% of owners use the funds to cover their operating expenses and 26% need them to refinance some other loans. It appears that loans play a huge part in the world of small businesses, as enterprises rely heavily on them both to keep afloat and make crucial steps towards the future.

11. 83.1% of US business owners started their companies.
(FactFinder)

In the true entrepreneurial spirit, 83.1% of owners built their companies from scratch. A significantly smaller percentage (11.3%) purchased their businesses, while 7.2% inherited them or received them as gifts.

12. Only 9% of entrepreneurs have a Bachelor's Degree in business.
(TSheets)

According to entrepreneurship data, an even smaller percentage of owners (3%) went beyond that with either a Master's Degree or a PhD in business. This is an important motivation for entrepreneurs who are only just starting out and worry about not having the proper education to pull it through. In fact, 32% of owners have only taken a couple of business classes, while most (46%) don't have any form of business education.

13. 26% of entrepreneurs turn to the internet for business-related advice.
(TSheets)

Quite logically, the internet is still one of the biggest resources for a small business owner. It contains plenty of official data that users might find useful. What's more, it gives them a chance to interact with each other and help each other out. In fact, entrepreneur statistics show 19% of business owners first turn to their colleagues for advice, while 14% go-to books for answers. Only 11% of respondents said they first turn to their family.

14. Studies show middle-aged men start the most successful businesses.
(MIT Sloan)

There is a belief that young people are responsible for most successful businesses out there. However, studies have shown that middle-aged men have a much better chance of succeeding in their enterprises, especially if they've already worked in the field before. Statistics about entrepreneurs tell us business owners who start their companies and hire at least one employee are 42 years of age on average.

15. Business and food are the two most popular industries for entrepreneurship.
(GuidantFinancial)

This is based on Guidant Financial data that lists 5 of the most popular industries. Business and food are at the top with 11%, followed by health/beauty with 10%, general retail (7%), and home services (6%). In 2018, the health and beauty industry saw a significant 34% rise thanks to the various related global trends. Food and business categories also saw a rise of 14%, while automotive businesses dropped from the top five spots.

Stats on Small Businesses

16. #1 reason why businesses fail is there's no market need.

(CBInsights)

According to the research done by CBInsights, 42% of businesses fail for this simple reason. The second most common reason that affects 29% of businesses is the lack of funds – in a word, bankruptcy. The third reason with 23% is the lack of chemistry and teamwork between employees.

17. 22.5% of small businesses fail in the first year.
(Office of Advocacy)

This is according to the new business statistics collected from 2004 to 2014. Calculations say only 79.9% of small businesses established in 2014 managed to get through to the next year. On average, about half of all companies survive more than 5 years, while only about a third reach the 10-year mark.

18. 60% of people who start small businesses are between the ages of 40 and 60.
(GuidantFinancial)

This is based on the 2019 small business study by Guidant Financial which surveyed more than 2,700 small entrepreneurship in the US. Interestingly enough, 4% of entrepreneurs were actually over 70 years of age. Clearly, it's never too late to start your own business.

19. 62% of small businesses don't have any staff.
(FreshBooks)

This stat makes sense considering a lot of entrepreneurs feel it's quite difficult to find the right, high-quality staff for their companies. Because of that, many decide to simply go solo. The same report shows 28% of businesses have 1-5 employees, while only 10% have over 5 employees.

20. In 2015, small business employment made around 45% of total private employment in the US.
(Office of Advocacy)

There were over 124,000 jobs in the private sector, compared to nearly 60,000 according to statistics on small businesses. The biggest share in individual industries agriculture and forestry, fishing & hunting with 85.1%. The smallest share of small businesses was in the company and enterprise management with 12.2%. Besides that, there were also 24,155 small business jobs not classified in any specific industry.

21. Small companies were responsible for 97.6% of exported goods in the US in 2015.
(Office of Advocacy)

In total, 295,834 companies exported goods from the US in 2015. Out of that number, 97.6% were actually small businesses, which amounts to 287,835 firms overall. Despite the sheer number of entrepreneurs in the US, these small businesses only earned 32.9% of the country's total export income – $1.3 trillion.

22. In a period of 21 years (from 1992 to 2013), small businesses accounted for 63.3% of new jobs in the US.
(Office of Advocacy)

It appears entrepreneurship is generally good for the economy of the whole country, as more than half of net new jobs came from these small businesses. In the aforementioned period, there were only two recessions, from 2001 to 2002 and 2007 to 2009, when the share was -47% and -61%, respectively.

23. Small businesses failure rate has declined by 30% since 1977.
(Entrepreneur)

These small business statistics are from Scott Shane, a professor at Case Western Reserve University. He argues this happened because business-owners are getting smarter, choosing profitable sectors and using reliable business-management technology. Apart from that, there is also a lower number of newly-created businesses and, therefore, less competition.

24. 67% of small business owners use personal funds to deal with various financial challenges.
(Federal Reserve Banks)

There are numerous financial challenges entrepreneurs face on a daily basis. The large majority decide to deal with them from their own pockets. Entrepreneurship statistics mention that 39% of owners prefer to take out an additional loan to deal with the crisis, while 33% take it out on the employees by cutting down the staff, hours, or downsizing their operations. Interestingly (or perhaps worryingly), 28% of owners simply choose to ignore their obligations.

25. 68% of small businesses have outstanding debt.
(Federal Reserve Banks)

A majority of enterprises are in debt, with 55% owing to less than $100,000. 37% of companies owe anywhere from $100k to $1 million, while 9% of companies owe over a million. This is according to an entrepreneur facts & statistics survey from 2017, although the outstanding debts seem to drag out from at least a year before.

26. Office of Advocacy statistics shows 60.1% of small businesses without paid employees are home-based.
(Federal Reserve Banks)

Many famous companies started off in their homes, garages, and basements. Stats show this is still the most popular location for small businesses and startups waiting for their big break. Of course, the situation changes when there are employees who demand certain working conditions, which is why only 23.3% of small employer firms are actually home-based.

Entrepreneur Statistics: Benefits and Challenges

27. 32% of business owners use cash to start their entrepreneurship.
(GuidantFinancial)

The second most popular way of funding small businesses for 13% of entrepreneurs is through their 401(k) retirement plan. On the other hand, 12% ask their friends and family for financial help, and 24% rely on various loans and credits. Crowdfunding seems to be the least popular option, with only 1% of owners deciding on it.

28. 55% of Americans believe they are able to start their own business.
(Babson)

This figure from startup statistics for 2016 represents the national average, but the numbers are even higher in cities like Miami (60%) and Detroit (57%). Quite understandably, in these cities, there is also a lower number of entrepreneurs who are afraid of failing. Only 27% of entrepreneurs in Miami and 21% in Detroit have a fear of failing compared to the national average of 33%.

29. The biggest challenge for 33% of small business owners is the lack of capital.
(GuidantFinancial)

Obviously, trying to make ends meet is no easy task, especially for small companies that are just starting out. That is why it makes sense that, according to statistics on small businesses, nearly a third of entrepreneurs feel they are barely staying afloat. For 15% of businesses, the greatest challenge is marketing – getting the company on the map, while 13% have a lot of problems with time management. Despite that fact, only 10% of entrepreneurs use outsourcing to help them with accounting. 17% outsource accounting, and 15% outsource payroll.

30. For 43% of employees, the biggest benefit of being self-employed is control over one's career.
(FreshBooks)

In that same sense, 43% of surveyed employees found in statistics on entrepreneurs say career change is a great motivator for turning away from traditional employment. 33% of the state the main reason why they would switch to self-employment is the financial incentive. While 32% of employees would start their own business for family reasons, 15% list health. They seem to believe being your own boss is less stressful or demanding and, therefore, better for your health.

31. 54% of self-employed entrepreneurs say they make more money now.
(FreshBooks)

This is something 67% of employees feel will happen once they've made the switch. 74% of employees feel they will also have to work harder when they become self-employed, but in reality, only 59% of entrepreneurs actually do so. The smallest difference in terms of expectations vs. reality of self-employment based on statistics about entrepreneurship is regarding work/life balance. 66% of people believe they will achieve it through entrepreneurship, and 68% of entrepreneurs confirm it.

32. 97% of self-employed professionals say they would never go back to traditional employment.
(FreshBooks)

If we look at these stats and compare them to previous ones, we can conclude that making the switch seems to be the biggest concern. Once it happens, a huge majority of employees feel satisfied with their choices. In addition to that, 70% of entrepreneurs work actively towards expanding their business, so there are certainly no regrets there.

33. For 27% of entrepreneurs, the hardest thing is to find talented staff or contractors.
(FreshBooks)

As you can imagine, making the switch from an employee to an employer comes with its own set of problems. US entrepreneurship statistics tell us that, besides finding quality workers, entrepreneurs also have problems with acquiring new customers (23%), finding money to reinvest (22%), setting the right prices (16%), and managing time effectively (15%). Interestingly, 17% of small business owners also mention one problem that people don't normally think about – not having enough cash in hand because it all goes through their company.

Minority-Owned Businesses

34. The majority of entrepreneurs in the US (64%) are white.(Babson)

14% are African-Americans, while 8% are Latino/Hispanic. Additionally, minority-owned business statistics for 2018 show the rates are a lot more stable among whites and least stable among African-Americans. This piece of information could signify that the white ethnicity is still privileged.

35. 61% of baby-boomers say they would work through retirement by choice.
(FreshBooks)

45% of millennials would do the same, as would 47% of employees who belong to gen X. Although it would appear that baby-boomers seem to be more into working post-retirement, the truth is their opinion might be affected by the fact they're either already retired or very nearly so. These startup statistics in 2018 numbers will undoubtedly change once gen X employees get closer to retirement.

36. For every 10 male entrepreneurs, there are 7 female entrepreneurs.
(Babson)

Around the world, there are 10 male entrepreneurs for every 7 female entrepreneurs. However, in six countries, this discrepancy has been all but ironed out, with women and men starting their own businesses at the same rate. These six countries are Indonesia, Thailand, Panama, Qatar, Madagascar, and Angola.

37. There are 8 million minority-owned businesses in the US.
(Office of Advocacy)

That being said, minority-owned businesses seem to hire fewer employees. In general, they have slightly over 8 employees, while non-minority owners hire more than 11 workers on average. The percentage of entrepreneurs in America shows us there's a substantial difference between men and women entrepreneurs. Male owners hire more than 12 employees on average, while female entrepreneurs hire slightly over 8 people.

38. Data from 2017 tells us there are an estimated 11.9 million small businesses in the US-owned by women.
(American Express)

These companies provide jobs for 9 million people and generate around $1.7 trillion in total. Over the course of 20 years, the number of female entrepreneurs has grown by 114%, which dramatically beats the total business growth rate of 44%. Furthermore, startup statistics show women-owned businesses make up 39% of all US companies.

39. Minorities accounted for 46% of women-owned businesses in the US in 2017.
(American Express)

There are around 5.5 million businesses owned by women who belong to minority groups. These enterprises employ more than 2.1 million people and generate $361 billion in revenue. African-American women make up 19% of the total women-owned businesses, Latinas own 17%, and Asian-American women own 9%.

FAQ

What percent of entrepreneurs are successful?

It depends on what you mean when you say successful. Entrepreneurship statistics show one-third of all companies manage to get through their 10th year, which can be considered quite a success. The large majority of successful entrepreneurs are actually middle-aged men who have been in the industry for quite some time.

What is the failure rate of all entrepreneurs?

Only 22.5% of small businesses close during their first year. Around half of all companies survive for at least 5 years, while a third of companies last for 10 years. This might seem like a scary piece of information, but the fact remains that nearly 80% of enterprises survive through their first year.

FINANCIAL FREEDOM

Personal Financial Success System

Our mission is to empower people to attain: Personal Financial Success

Personal Financial Success is simply having enough cash flow to support our lifestyles during our working years and our retirement years.

To attain Personal Financial Success, we need to earn enough cash flow during our working years to support our lifestyles and simultaneously invest enough money to build enough assets to generate our desired retirement income. Example: If someone is earning $100,000 annually during their working years, they will need at least 12 times that annual amount or about $1,200,000 in their investment account.

.America is the wealthiest country in the world, accounting for over 25% of the world's wealth. America has over 12 million millionaires, and over 1000 people become millionaires in America every day, but even with all this wealth millions of Americans are struggling financially. So, the question is, why? There are many reasons, but, the number one reason is the strategy people use to create their income and wealth. America is a capitalistic country, which means the biggest financial rewards go to business owners and investors. Unfortunately, most Americans are not business owners and do very little investing. Fortunately, we have a solution.

Our Solution Is

- "More Cash flow & Smart Financial Strategies". You might be thinking, how can More Cash flow & Smart Financial Strategies help me attain financial success? Think about what an additional $1000 or more in monthly cash flow could do for your budget. You could pay off debt quickly, build investments faster or even enhance your lifestyle.

- We have two powerful methods for associates to acquire more cash flow.

- The first method is using strategies in our Income Shifting Membership. The membership has 5 cash flow strategies which enable associates to acquire additional cash flow by restructuring their current finances.

- The second method is by Earning Business Income referring the membership to other people.

Let's discuss how we increase our cash flow using the strategies in the membership first.

Smart Cash flow Strategies

The first strategy is Correct Tax Withholding - The IRS says over 100 million employees have too much money withheld from their paychecks for taxes. When too much money is withheld for taxes, employees lose money because they could have used that money for investing, debt elimination or lifestyle. Every day, we help hundreds of people correct their W4 and increase their take-home pay by hundreds of dollars monthly.

The 2nd strategy is to Minimize Taxes. As an Associate, you become a business owner. Business owners have access to many more tax deductions than employees. Those deductions can save business owners thousands of dollars. We provide each associate with our cashflow manager app, which tracks income, expenses, receipts and business miles. We also provide training from the IRS website on potential deductions and how to document them.

Our 3rd strategy is Debt Elimination. We provide each associate with: Debt Elimination Software, Debt Elimination Training, and Extra Cashflow to eliminate debt fast.

The 4th Strategy is Build Great Credit - Our myCredit System provides each associate educational videos and support tools to build a great credit score. Associates learn how to dispute negative credit history and how to maximize credit utilization, credit mix, credit history, and new credit.

Our fifth strategy, Investment Education leads to investment income which provides Financial Freedom. We provide training on Investment Terminology and Investment Strategies. One of our most important strategies is Own A Piece of America. As consumers, we spend millions of dollars during our lifetime with big American companies, shifting some of those dollars into buying stock in those companies instead of consumer goods only, simply makes sense. Our associates increase their cash flow using the strategies in the membership and earn business income referring the membership to other people.

World Class Compensation Plan

•We have a World Class Compensation Plan. The system is World Class because we pay every Friday and we make money by simply enrolling members into our inexpensive membership and asking those members to refer the membership to other people. Every time a new member enrolls: You earn upfront weekly income & monthly residual income.

•You earn up to $40.00 on personal enrollees and up to $30.00 on team enrollees to infinity. After your first enrollee, you can refer a friend and earn $40.00, that friend can refer a friend and you earn $30.00, this can go on to infinity. Imagine having 25, 50 or even 100 new members enroll on your team weekly. Top Associates earn thousands of dollars in weekly commissions.

•You also earn up to $8 monthly residual income on each active membership.

Let's look at the income potential.

World Class Compensation Plan

•If your team enrolls 10 new members weekly, you earn up to $400 in upfront weekly income, in 12 months you could have 500 active members and be earning an additional $3500 in monthly residual income

- If your team enrolls 50 new members weekly, you earn up to $2000 in upfront weekly income, in 12 months you could have 2500 active members and be earning an additional $40,000 in monthly residual income

- If your team enrolls 250 new members weekly, you earn up to $10,000 in upfront weekly income, in 12 months you could have 12,500 active members and be earning an additional $100,000 in monthly residual income

- In addition to weekly commissions and monthly residual income on memberships, you also earn 50% on personal retail product sales and up to 25% on team retail product sales. You simply refer customers to the website and get paid. Some of our key products are our:

- **Cash back Mall** which has over 1000 stores and millions of products

- **Discount Travel** for most major brands and our

- **Identity Theft Protection with Free & Discount Legal Services included**

Thousands of people have increased their cash flow using the systems and have made us one of the fastest-growing companies in America. Let's look at one of our best points, the price. When you sign up, you get. . .

Sign Up and Receive

✓ A Personalized Website, Our Income Shifting Membership and Our

World-Class Business System: Our membership includes:

✓ Our Tax Withholding Training . . . . . .

✓ Our Cash flow Manager, Tax Record Keeping App The Debt Elimination System . . . our

myCredit, credit building system . . . and

Our Investment Education Training

✓ ✓ ✓ ✓ Because of our special promotion, you can get started for a onetime fee of just $49.95 and

then a small monthly fee of just $34.95 beginning 30 days after enrollment.

✓ Remember the fees are tax-deductible and as an actively engaged business owner, you can

get thousands of dollars in tax deductions.

Inbox or Call Adolph (910) 514-3448
www.incomeshifting.com

IM HELPING
300 PEOPLE
RESTORE THEIR CREDIT
GOING INTO
2020

www.adolphmoore.com

Get started today & start making and saving money immediately!!!

SIGN UP TODAY @ www.adolphmoore.com

IF YOU HAVE ANY QUESTIONS PLEASE FEEL FREE TO CALL ME @ 910-514-3448

EMAIL: adolphmoore71@gmail.com

IMAGINE YOUR CHURCH HAVING THIS SYSTEM. THE CHURCH CAN GET RESIDUAL INCOME.

FOR THE 5 MINUTE VIDEO
www.incomeshifting.com

FOR THE 20 MINUTE VIDEO

www.maximumcashflow.com

BUSINESS OPPORTUNITIES

#1 MyEcon page 68- 74

www.6figureswithadolph.com

#2 Easy1up

https://easy1up.com/?id=adolphmoore

www.paidnstyle.com

This is an International Business Opportunity that is still a home based business. Click Join Now on the page to get started..

#3 Abundance Network

https://salesrobot.ai/ava/?ref=adolphmoore

www.mailboxcash123.com

or Call Ava the robot for info **386-518-0304**

This a automated system where you can total work from your phone with SMS systems.

#4 Mailbox Cash
https://www.clubcashfund.com/adolphmoore71

www.mailboxcash24.com

This is a Direct Mail online and offline business opportunity that brings cash directly to your home.

#5 Lead Lightning Affiliate

www.cashonoffline.com

#6 Foreign Exchange Trading (Tradera)

http://bit.ly/Forex_Overview

http://bit.ly/Forex_Tradera_Payplan

FACEBOOK GROUP

http://bit.ly/Forex_Cash_Fun

TO SIGN UP

http://bit.ly/Forex_Adolph

www.ingramcontent.com/pod-product-compliance
Lightning Source LLC
Chambersburg PA
CBHW031212090426
42736CB00009B/888